Wit and

The Second Time Around

Large Type Edition

Published by
The National Federation
of the Blind

Printed in the United States of America

Table of Contents

Introduction

Two years ago, I complied with the wishes of many of our NFB members by putting together a compilation of the jokes and funny stories that have appeared in the National Federation of the Blind "Presidential Message" tapes over the years. I started the practice of including a touch of humor at the end of these tapes in 1968. I did this because the "Presidential Messages" were always filled with the serious problems of blindness, and I wanted to share these jokes and funny stories with my friends...to take our minds off the problems of blindness and to lighten the day's burden with a little fun.

This second edition of jokes and funny stories, WIT AND WITTICISM THE SECOND TIME AROUND, is due in large part to the many letters of thanks and encouragement we have received from people all over the country who enjoyed reading that book—THE BELL, THE CLAPPER, AND THE CORD: WIT AND WITTICISM.

I hope that in some small way our books will make your day better by making you smile and forget your daily problems...even for just a few minutes.

Kenneth Jernigan
President Emeritus

Why Large Type

The type size in this book is 14 point for two important reasons: One, because typesetting of 14 point or larger complies with federal standards for the printing of materials for visually impaired readers, and we want to show you exactly what type size is necessary for people with limited sight.

The second reason is that many of our friends and supporters have asked us to print our paperback books in 14-point type so they too can easily read them. Many people with limited sight do not use Braille. We hope that by printing this book in a larger type than customary, many more people will be able to benefit from it.

Kenneth Jernigan, *President Emeritus*
National Federation of the Blind

Some Things Never Change

There are certain laughter-evoking phrases and lines that have been around as long as many of us began sharing jokes among ourselves and our friends. The origin of some of these jokes cannot be attributed to the provider so read and enjoy!

Did you hear about what they said regarding the candidate's speech at the political convention?

The longer the spoke, the bigger the tire.

Why was Cinderella a poor basketball player?

Because she had a pumpkin for a coach.

Here is a wise old saying—Christmas is a holiday when neither the past nor the future is as interesting as the present.

What do you call advice given to a blind traveler?

A cane tip.

What is the difference between in-laws and outlaws?

Outlaws are wanted.

The baby light bulb said to the mama light bulb, "I wuv you watts."

Why are banks called money trees?

Because they have so many branches.

This coffee's awfully muddy.

Well, it ought to be. It was ground yesterday.

What is it that's white and green and Irish and only comes out in the summer?

Why, it's Paddy O'Furniture.

Did you hear about the cat that swallowed a ball of yarn and had mittens?

Time flies like an arrow; fruit flies like bananas.

When are sheep like ink?

When they're in a pen.

What is the difference between an elephant and a flea?

An elephant can have fleas but a flea can't have elephants.

How do you get down from an elephant?

You don't get down from an elephant; you get down from a goose.

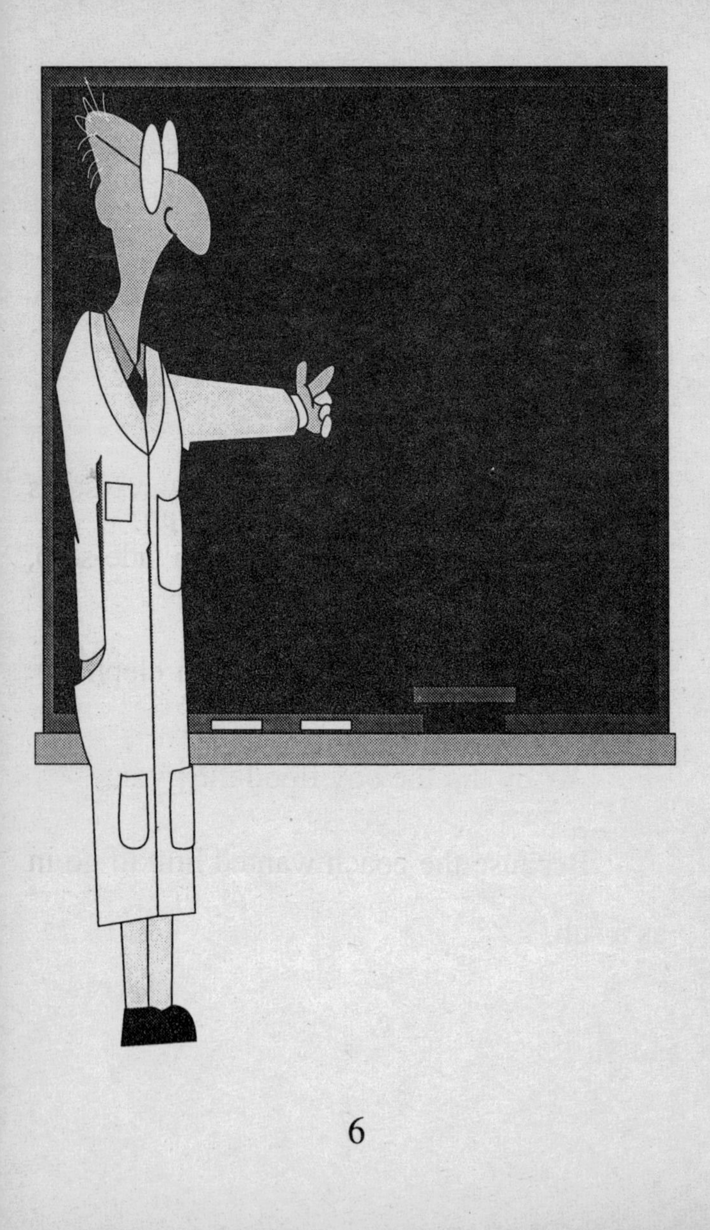

It's Academic

There was a dance teacher who talked of a very old dance called the Politician.

You do this dance by taking three steps forward, two steps backward, then side-step, side-step, and turn around.

Why did the boy flood the gym?

Because the coach wanted him to go in as a sub.

Little Sammy was practicing his violin in the living room while his father was trying to read his newspaper in the den. The family dog was lying in front of the father, and as the screeching sounds of the youngster's violin playing reached the pup's ears, he began to howl dismally. The father endured the violin and the dog as long as he could. Finally he jumped up and slammed his paper to the floor and yelled above the din, "For pity's sake, can't you play something the dog doesn't know?!"

What did one mountain say to the other after the earthquake?

It's not my fault.

What did the ocean say to the beach?

Nothing. It just waved.

What's the difference between a school teacher and a train?

The teacher says, "Spit out your gum." And the train says, "Chew, chew, chew."

Did you hear about the English teacher who has a snowman in her class?

She had to flunk him because he couldn't get the drift.

What kind of publication should a gardener read?

The Weeder's Digest.

What is the encyclopedia?

A fine-couthed tome.

What word has the most letters in it?

Why, a mailbox.

A reader and a writer went into the jungle and they encountered a lion. Which did the lion eat?

Well, the reader of course, because you have writer's cramp and reader's digest.

What did the billy goat say after he ate the film?

The book was better.

If con is the opposite of pro, do you know what the opposite of progress is?

Do I need to tell you? Congress.

Do you know why Cleopatra said, "No!"

Because she was the queen of denial.

What famous noon meal was invented by a composer?

Bach's lunch.

How many hired hands does it take to change a light bulb?

Many of them, for many hands make light work.

Why do fluorescent lights hum?

Because they don't know the words.

What did the limestone deposit say to the geologist?

You must stop taking me for granite.

A cat has its claws at the end of its paws and a comma has its pause at the end of a clause.

When is a sailor no longer a sailor?

When he's aboard.

Old bankers never die. They just lose interest.

What bird is the most contented?

Of course, the crow. He never complains without caws.

Healthful Hints

Medical terms have been defined and redefined throughout history. Here are some offerings that may bring new meaning to the mystery of medical science.

Do you know how long people should stay in a hospital bed?

The same amount of time as short people do.

Why do surgeons make good comedians?

Because they always leave you in stitches.

How will you feel after surgery?

Just sew-sew.

What is the difference between a medicine bottle and a door mat?

One is taken up and shaken, the other is shaken up and taken.

Did you hear about the man who decided to walk a mile a day but found a short cut that would let him do it in five blocks?

The doctor said, “How is the boy who swallowed the half dollar?” The nurse said, “No change yet.”

How many psychiatrists does it take to change a light bulb?

Only one, but the light bulb has to really want to change.

Did you hear about the man who went to the doctor to complain that he felt like a deck of cards? The doctor said, "Sit down and I'll deal with you later."

Did you hear about the duck who went to the drugstore and asked the pharmacist to give him a chapstick and put it on his bill?

How do you mend a broken heart?

With ticker tape.

What two letters are your teeth afraid of?

Of course, D-K.

What do you call an unnatural fear of Christmas?

Claus-trophobia.

Why didn't the skeleton go to the dance?

Because he had no body to go with.

DON'T

The Employee's Handbook

What did they give the person who invented the door knocker?

The no-bell prize.

What does a bee suffer from if he visits too many flowers?

High bud pressure.

Why did the man in the orange juice factory lose his job?

He couldn't concentrate.

The lady in the optometrist's office stepped before the doctor who said, "Eyes checked?" She said, "No, they're blue."

Did you hear about the fellow who invested in a paper towel company and a revolving door company? He was wiped out before he could turn around.

What did the adding machine say to the cashier?

"You can count on me."

Old auctioneers never die. They just look forbidding.

Why do policemen have such nice looking yards?

Because they keep law'n order.

When the seamstress asked the weatherman if he wanted his trousers cut long or short, he said that he'd like to have them fair-in-height.

Why did the bow-legged cowboy get fired?

Because he couldn't keep his calves together.

Somewhere Between the Barn and the Vegetable Patch

The history of humor would not be complete without its references to vegetables, farm and zoo animals, and their activities. These may inspire some of your own contributions.

What do you call a dog with no legs?

It doesn't really matter, it won't come anyway.

What do you use to mend a jack-o-lantern?

Why, of course, a pumpkin patch.

I called my dog multiplier because he had one sore leg. All the time he would put down three and carry the one.

Did you hear that round hay bales have been outlawed? It was because the cows were not getting a square meal.

What do you get if you cross a lighthouse with a hen house?

Beacon and eggs.

Why are pigs always ready for accidents?

They have spare ribs.

How can you stop a dog from barking in the back yard?

Let him go out front.

Why did the little pig leave home?

Because his father was such an awful boar.

What do you call the condition of a cow which makes it unable to give milk?

Udder failure.

Why did the radish kiss the banana?

Because the banana had a peel.

Why is a field of grass always older than you are?

Because it's pasture age.

What do you call a cow with two legs that are shorter than the other two?

Lean beef.

Where do frogs hang their coats?

Of course, in the croakroom.

Why did the chicken cross the road?

Doubtless, it was for some fowl reason.

Why did the unwashed chicken cross the road twice?

Because he was a dirty double-crosser.

Why did the chicken stop in the middle of the road?

So she could lay it on the line.

Culture Shock

What do you call a nun who walks in her sleep?

A Roman catholic.

What time did God create Adam?

A little before Eve.

Did you hear about the vampire who first joined but then quit the vegetarian club?

He learned that you can't get blood out of a turnip.

What kinds of ghosts haunt skyscrapers?

High spirits.

Why did the Indians live here first?

Because they had reservations.

Why was Adam the fastest runner?

Because he was the first in the human race.

Why didn't Adam and Eve use computers and calculators?

Because the Lord said to multiply on the face of the earth.

What do you call a knife that can slice through four loaves of bread?

A four loaf cleaver.

What do you call a group of mushrooms that go to a bar and buy drinks for everybody?

Fun guys.

What did the bald man say when he was given a comb?

I'll never part with it.

How do you flatten a ghost?

You use a spirit level.

Why do they build fences around cemeteries?

Because people are dying to get in.

Do you know where Martians go fishing?

In the galaxy.

Here is a sign on the back of a hearse:

If you're out of time, we've got the bier.

Why was six afraid of seven?

Because seven eight nine.

Did you hear about the cannibal who liked to eat where they served truck drivers?

What do an English slot machine and a Weight Watcher's diet have in common?

They're both designed to help you lose pounds.

What is to be more admired than a promising young man?

Well, of course, a paying one.

Why do you always put your left shoe on last?

Well, because when you put on one shoe, the other is left.

Life in the Fast Lane

How do you find out how many spokes there are in a bicycle wheel?

Why, ask a spokesperson.

It seems that the Leaning Tower of Pisa and the tower of Big Ben were thinking of planning a family. But they couldn't, they had to call it off. One of them didn't have the time, and the other didn't have the inclination.

Why did the lady put lipstick on her forehead?

She wanted to make up her mind.

What kind of corsage should you give Lassie?

The one made out of collie flowers.

Did you hear about the man who told his neighbor while he was polishing his car, "I get about seven miles per gallon from this car. My son gets the other twenty."

If you have a bee in your hand, what do you have in your eye?

Why beauty, because beauty is in the eye of the bee holder.

Why do bees buzz?

Well, wouldn't you buzz if somebody took your honey and necked her?

What did the bee say as it approached the hive?

"Hi, home, I'm honey."

What do canoes and small children have in common?

They both work better when paddled from behind.

There was a waiter who came by with a steak and the indignant customer said, "You've got your thumb on my steak!" And the waiter said, "I didn't want it to fall on the floor again."

Why did the hungry baseball fan with the ice cold hot dogs raise his hand high and wriggle his little finger?

Because he wanted to have a microwave.

What do you get when you have a cold puppy sitting on a rabbit?

Chilly dog on a bunny.

Where do moths dance?

At the moth ball.

What is despair?

Da tire you keep in da trunk of da car.

Why did the man drive his car off the cliff?

Because he wanted to test his air brakes.

What is the difference between a mouse and a young lady?

One harms the cheese and one charms the he's.

Why is a room full of married couples much like an empty room?

There isn't a single person in the place.

What is red and goes beep-beep?

A strawberry in a traffic jam.

Conditions of Employment

Did you hear about the fight between the dentist and the manicurist?

They went at it tooth and nail.

What do you call two dentists?

A pairadocs.

There were two rehabilitation counselors, Elmer and Larry, out hunting in the woods who got lost. Elmer was panicky so Larry said to him, "Don't worry, all we have to do is shoot three times into the air and someone will come to rescue us." Which they did. But nobody came. They tried it again, and nobody came. Finally, Larry said, "Elmer, I'm getting kind of worried. We're down to our last three arrows."

Did you hear about the glass blower who inhaled and got a pane in his stomach?

Is a telephone operator engaged in a business or a profession?

Neither, in a calling.

Old salesmen never die, they just get out of commission.

Old accountants never die, they just lose their balance.

Creatures Great and Small

What is the smartest insect in the world?

A bookworm.

Why did the children play kick the pebble?

Because it was too hard to play kick the boulder.

What do you get when you cross a rabbit with a spider?

A hare net.

Why did the pig flee from the medical school?

He learned that when it comes to pork, first you kill them, then you cure them.

How many hairs does a rabbit have in its tail?

None, they are all on the outside.

Why should you never tell a pig a secret?

Because it's a squealer.

Did you hear about the exhausted kangaroo?

He was out of bounds.

What does the Easter bunny get for a basket?

Two points, the same as everybody else.

What did the porcupine say to the cactus?

Is that you, mother?

What is an octopus?

A cat that only has eight of its lives left.

What do you get when you cross an alarm clock with a German shepherd?

A watch dog.

What happens when a frog is parked illegally?

It's toad away.

What do you get when you cross a dachshund with a zebra?

Striped sausages.

What did the rabbit say when it jumped into its hole which was full of water?

Oh, well.

The snake charmer got a present to keep around his neck. It was a boa tie.

Why was the lady rabbit so unhappy?

She had a bad hare day.

How do you tune a fish?

You have to know the scale.

What animal eats with its tail?

They all do. They can't take them off.

What should you do if you catch your dog eating the dictionary?

Take the words right out of its mouth.

What do a dog and the forest have in common?

There's a lot of bark in both.

What do you get when you manicure a buffalo?

A bison toenail.

I call my little dog Hardware because when he hears his name he bolts for the door.

What do you get when a duck flies upside down?

You get a quack-up.

What happens if you cross a pigeon with a zero?

You get a flying none.

Is a dog better dressed in the summer, or in the winter?

He's better dressed in the summer because in the winter he has a coat, but in the summer he has a coat and pants.

What do you call a rabbit that hasn't been out of the house?

It's an ingrown hare.

Did you hear about the cat who ate cheese and sat by the mouse hole with baited breath?

Or have you heard the sheep song?

There'll never be another ewe.

Do you know why the farmer called his pig Ink?

Because he always kept running out of the pen.

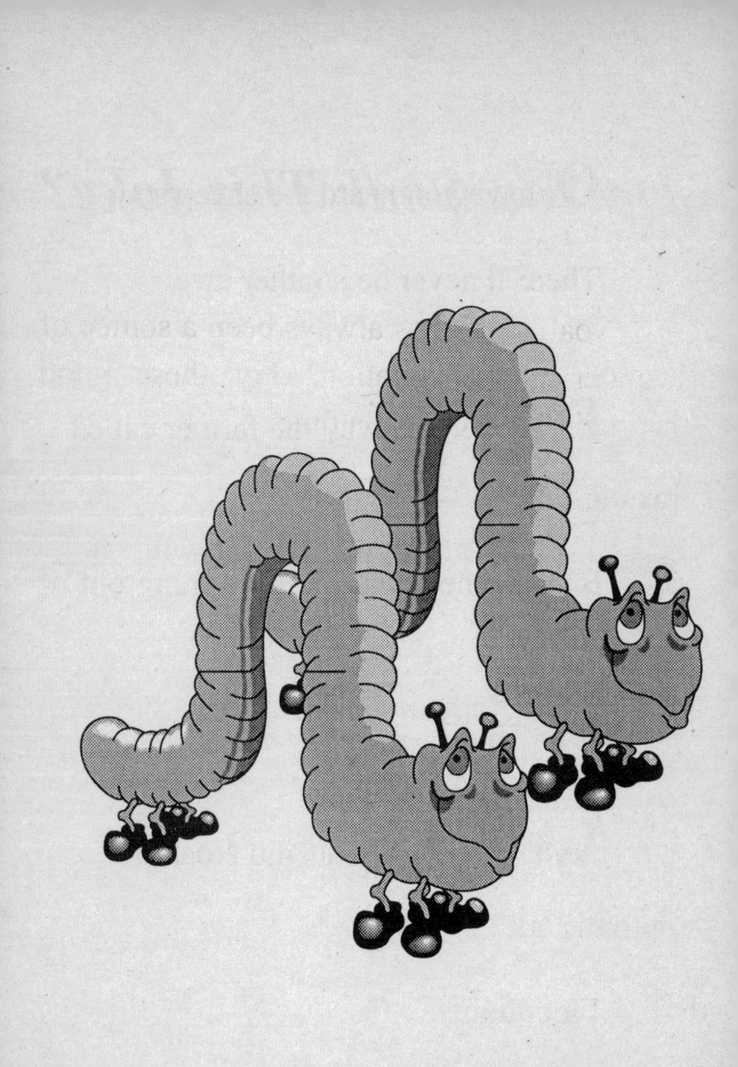

Do You Noah This Joke?

Noah's Ark has always been a source of wonder and inspiration. Try these good hearted riddles two at a time.

Did Noah do much fishing while he was on the Ark?

No, he only had two worms.

What kind of lights did Noah put onto the ark?

Floodlights.

Why is it that the animals on Noah's Ark couldn't eat apples?

Because they went aboard in pears.

One day a friend visited my granddad and asked him if he knew that Arkansas was the only state mentioned in the Bible.

Noah looked out of the Ark and Saw the dove.

Why was there no card playing on the Ark?

Because Noah was sitting on the deck.

A Special Kind of Wisdom

What driver never gets arrested for speeding?

A screwdriver.

How many coins can you put into an empty piggy bank?

Only one, after that the piggy bank isn't empty anymore.

If birds that fly over the sea are seagulls, then birds that fly over the bay are baygulls?

Did you hear about the two bed bugs who fell in love and were married in the spring?

She heard on television that brushing alone won't prevent cavities. Think of all the people who always brush alone, what will they do?

What kind of weather is there when it rains oodles of cats?

A downpurr.

How can you tell a dogwood tree?

By its bark.

Which is the better baseball team, the Red Sox or the Nylons?

You may like the Red Sox, but the Nylons get more runs.

What is the world's largest punctuation mark?

It's the hundred yard dash.

What kind of mail is best to get on a hot summer day?

Fan mail.

What kind of person steals soap?

A dirty crook.

What begins and ends with "e," but has only one letter?

An envelope.

How do you get rid of a boomerang?

Throw it down a one-way street.

What two things can you never eat for breakfast?

Lunch and dinner.

If the last one didn't send you, try this: Did you hear about the man who always wore a watch in his back pocket so that he would never be behind time?

Do you know who was the only man in the world who ever got all of his work done by Friday?

Well, of course, it was Robinson Crusoe.

Do you know the definition of a vitamin?

It's what you do when a friend comes to your door.

Did you hear about the hurricane that lost its force and was disgusted?

Or, do you know what happens when you haven't worked a field for a long time?

The land is distilled.

A motorist was going the wrong way on a one way street, and a cop stopped him and said: Look buster, where do you think you're going? And the motorist looked up and said: Oh, well it's okay, officer, I guess

I'm too late anyway. I see everybody's coming back.

Did you hear about the shipload of paint that wrecked and marooned all the sailors?

Riddles Galore

What did the boy volcano say to the girl volcano?

Do you lava me like I lava you?

What is a bee called that keeps dropping things?

A bumble bee.

Why don't chickens have trunks?

Because they never go on vacation.

Why is baseball like pancakes?

They both depend on the batter.

Why don't cannibals eat comedians?

Because they taste funny.

Why did the lion cross the jungle?

To get to the other pride.

Why did the ship cross the ocean?

To get to the other tide.

When is it bad luck for a black cat to follow you?

When you're a mouse.

How do you know if a cat burglar has been in your house?

If the cat is missing.

Why did the chicken coup only have two doors?

If it had four doors, it would be a sedan.

What do you get when you cross a turkey with a whale?

A Christmas dinner that needs tons of stuffing.

Did you hear about the chicken that swallowed the racing form?

Now she's laying odds.

Why was the man staring fixedly at the orange juice?

The sign on the can said, "concentrate."

If you throw a red ball into the blue Danube, what will it become?

Wet.

Why should you never use hair oil before taking a test?

All the facts will slip your mind.

From the Peanut Gallery

We have received many favorable letters in response to the publication of our first book of wit, *The Bell, The Clapper, and the Cord: Wit and Witticism.* A number of these included jokes and riddles that we want to share with all our friends.

Did you hear about the Big Hold Up?

Two clothespins held up a man's pants.

Jake: My new jeans are tighter than my skin.

Joe: How do you know?

Jake: Well, I can sit down in my skin, but I can't in my jeans.

What do you call a person who crosses the ocean twice and never takes a bath?

A Dirty Double Crosser.

A doctor prescribed to his patient that he walk two miles daily. A month later the patient called the doctor and said, "I'm in Philadelphia. What should I do now?"

Horse sense is stable thinking coupled with the ability to say "Nay."

Giant oak trees started out as little nuts that held their ground.

An older man was telling his friends that he was getting married; they asked:

Can she cook? No.

Is she pretty? Not really.

Is she wealthy? No.

Why are you marrying her?

She can drive at night.

Love: An ocean of emotions entirely surrounded by expenses.

It's foolish to work up a head of steam unless you know what's cooking.

How come the man tiptoed past the medicine cabinet?

He didn't want to wake the sleeping pills.

What if everyone drove a red car, what would we have?

A red car nation.

Three things a skier needs: Green money, White snow, and Blue Cross.

When is a dog's tail not a tail?

When it's a wagon.

National Federation of the Blind

You can help us spread the word...

...about our Braille Readers Are Leaders contest for blind schoolchildren, a project which encourages blind children to achieve literacy through Braille.

...about our scholarships for deserving blind college students.

...about Job Opportunities for the Blind, a program that matches capable blind people with employers who need their skills.

...about where to turn for accurate information about blindness and the abilities of the blind.

Most importantly, you can help us by sharing what you've learned about blindness in these pages with your family and friends. If you know anyone who needs assistance with the problems of blindness, please write:

Marc Maurer, President
1800 Johnson Street, Suite 300
Baltimore, Maryland 21230-4998

Your contribution is tax-deductible.